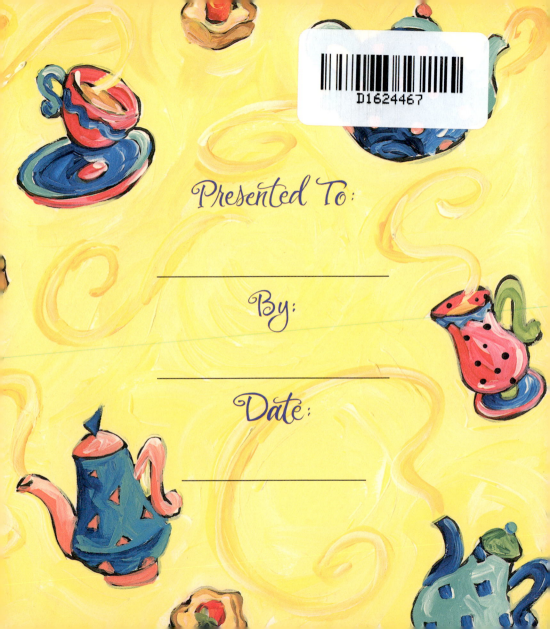

D1624467

Presented To:

_____

By:

_____

Date:

_____

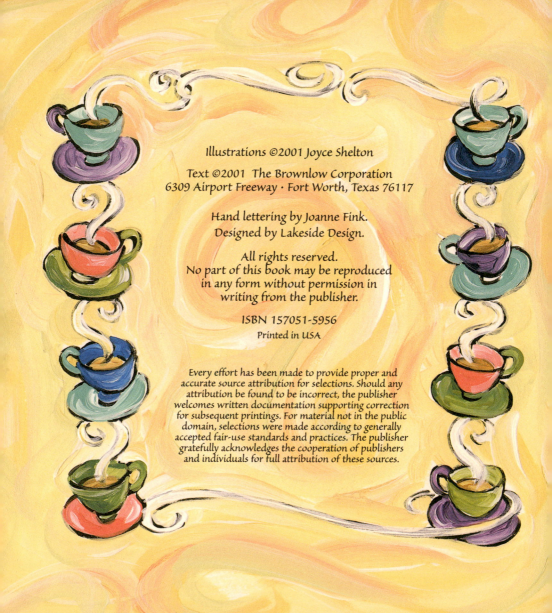

Illustrations ©2001 Joyce Shelton

Text ©2001 The Brownlow Corporation
6309 Airport Freeway · Fort Worth, Texas 76117

Hand lettering by Joanne Fink.
Designed by Lakeside Design.

All rights reserved.
No part of this book may be reproduced
in any form without permission in
writing from the publisher.

ISBN 157051-5956
Printed in USA

Every effort has been made to provide proper and
accurate source attribution for selections. Should any
attribution be found to be incorrect, the publisher
welcomes written documentation supporting correction
for subsequent printings. For material not in the public
domain, selections were made according to generally
accepted fair-use standards and practices. The publisher
gratefully acknowledges the cooperation of publishers
and individuals for full attribution of these sources.

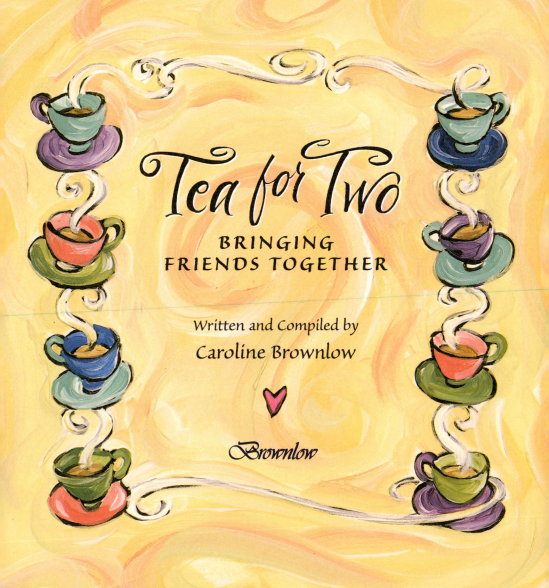

Tea for Two

BRINGING FRIENDS TOGETHER

Written and Compiled by
Caroline Brownlow

Brownlow

Tea for Two

Originally the phrase, "tea for two", was an English street cry in the eighteenth century that vendors used to advertise their bargain-priced tea. Normally a pot of tea was *thruppence* (three pence), but enterprising souls hungry for more business would often lower it to *tuppence* (two pence), by shouting, "Tea for two!"

Today the phrase has come to mean so much more. It now speaks of a cozy time for friends to relax, to enjoy the moment, unburden themselves for an hour or two, and share their lives together.

Not Your Mother's Cup of Tea

*W*hile drinking tea has been around for thousands
of years, it is a currently going through a quiet
revolution. Tea sales more than doubled from
1990 to 1998 and the trend is growing.

For years, tea has somehow been associated with proper
British ladies, ornate tearooms and dainty little sandwiches.
And while these traditions will continue for some people,
tea is shedding its social stereotypes:

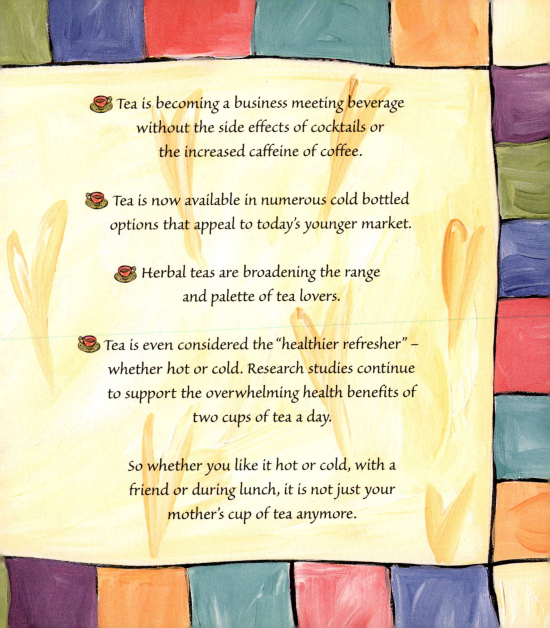

Tea is becoming a business meeting beverage without the side effects of cocktails or the increased caffeine of coffee.

Tea is now available in numerous cold bottled options that appeal to today's younger market.

Herbal teas are broadening the range and palette of tea lovers.

Tea is even considered the "healthier refresher" – whether hot or cold. Research studies continue to support the overwhelming health benefits of two cups of tea a day.

So whether you like it hot or cold, with a friend or during lunch, it is not just your mother's cup of tea anymore.

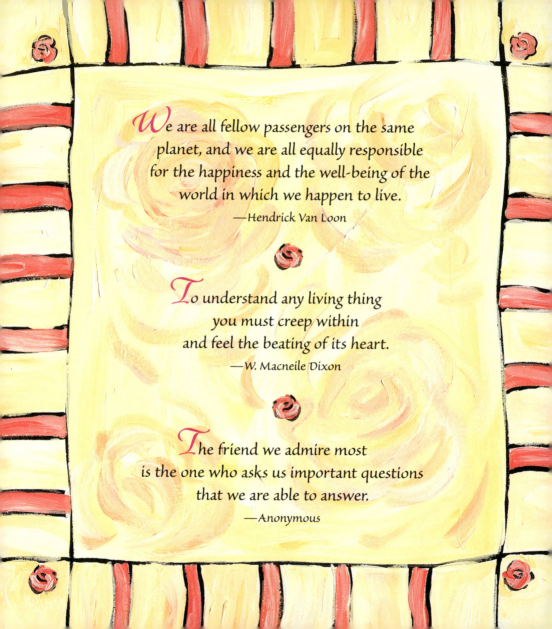

*W*e are all fellow passengers on the same
planet, and we are all equally responsible
for the happiness and the well-being of the
world in which we happen to live.

—Hendrick Van Loon

*T*o understand any living thing
you must creep within
and feel the beating of its heart.

—W. Macneile Dixon

*T*he friend we admire most
is the one who asks us important questions
that we are able to answer.

—Anonymous

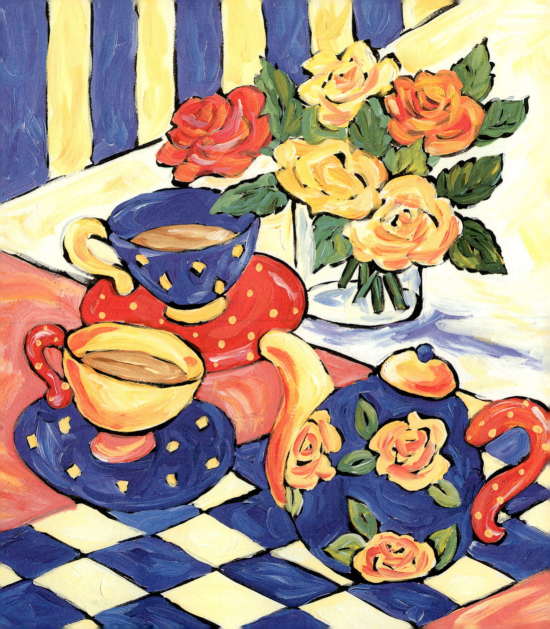

There can be no real and abiding happiness without sacrifice. Our greatest joys do not result from our efforts toward self-gratification, but from a loving and spontaneous service to other lives. Joy comes not to him who seeks it for himself, but to him who seeks it for other people.

—H. W. Sylvester

Nothing is ever lost by courtesy. It is the cheapest of the pleasures; costs nothing and conveys much. It pleases him who gives and him who receives, and thus, like mercy, it is twice blessed.

—Erastus Wiman

The happiness of life is made up of minute fractions – the little soon forgotten charities of a kiss or smile, a kind look, a heartfelt compliment, and the countless infinitesimals of pleasurable and genial feeling.

—Samuel Taylor Coleridge

Like China

The finest china in the world is burned at least
three times, some of it more than three times.
Dresden china is always burned three times.
Why does it go through that intense fire?

Once ought to be enough; twice ought to be enough.
No, three times are necessary to burn that china so
that the gold and the crimson are brought out more
beautiful and then fastened there to
stay. We are fashioned after the
same principle in human life. Our
trials are burned into us one,
twice, thrice; and by God's
grace these beautiful colors are
there and they are
there to stay forever.

—Cortland Myers

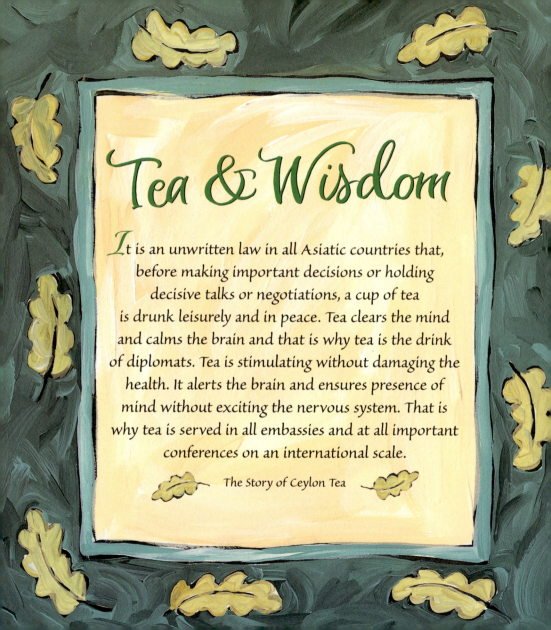

Tea & Wisdom

It is an unwritten law in all Asiatic countries that, before making important decisions or holding decisive talks or negotiations, a cup of tea is drunk leisurely and in peace. Tea clears the mind and calms the brain and that is why tea is the drink of diplomats. Tea is stimulating without damaging the health. It alerts the brain and ensures presence of mind without exciting the nervous system. That is why tea is served in all embassies and at all important conferences on an international scale.

The Story of Ceylon Tea

*T*wo are better than one. If one falls down, his friend can help him up. But pity the man who falls and has no one to help him up!

—Ecclesiastes 4:9-10

*W*e can win more friends with our ears than with our mouths.

—Anonymous

*N*ever place a period where God has placed a comma.

—Gracie Allen

A Cool Reception

Iced tea was created in America nearly 100 years ago, so perhaps it is only fitting that America is the only country where the majority of tea is enjoyed cold. In fact, iced tea was invented because visitors to the 1904 St. Louis World's Fair were not interested in drinking hot tea on a hot, summer day. The hot tea was getting a cool reception. Therefore, quick-thinking English tea merchant Richard Blechynden added ice, and the rest is history.

Today 80 percent of the 2.2 billion gallons of tea consumed by Americans each year is served cold. Iced tea is so popular that each year June is celebrated as National Iced Tea Month.

So What is Tea, Really?

Indigenous to China, Tibet and Northern India, the tea plant (Camellia sinensis) is a shrubby evergreen. Left alone, it grows to 30 feet and bears fragrant white flowers. Tea planters prune it to three to five feet for convenience in harvesting. The best teas are grown in mountains to 6,000 feet. Perfect conditions for the flavor and quality include an average shade temperature of 65° and well-distributed rainfall of 100 inches a year, with long intervals of sun in-between showers. Now, three-fourths of the world's tea comes from India and Sri Lanka. It also grows in Java and Formosa, as well as in china and Tibet. The delightful beverage is made from the dried leaves.

Tea & Friendship

A true friend is one who sticks by you
even when she gets to know you real well.

—Anonymous

Friendship above all ties does bind the heart,
And faith in friendship is the noblest part.

—Lord Orrery

A true friend thinks of you when all others
are thinking of themselves.

—Anonymous

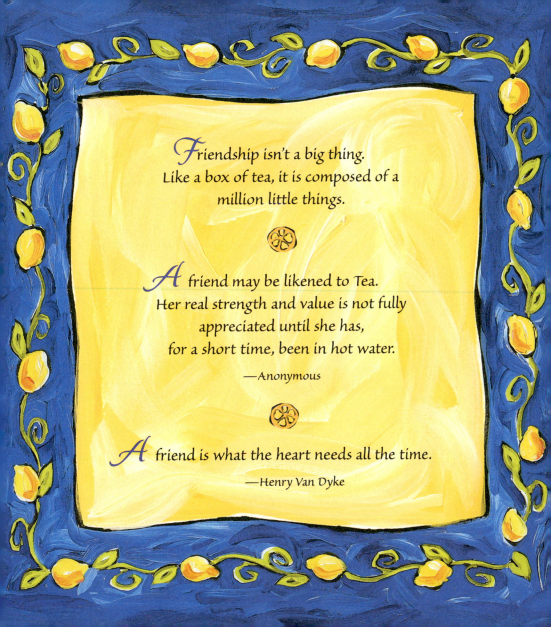

*F*riendship isn't a big thing.
Like a box of tea, it is composed of a
million little things.

A friend may be likened to Tea.
Her real strength and value is not fully
appreciated until she has,
for a short time, been in hot water.

—Anonymous

A friend is what the heart needs all the time.

—Henry Van Dyke

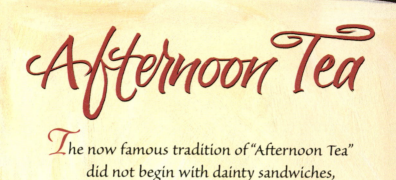

Afternoon Tea

The now famous tradition of "Afternoon Tea"
did not begin with dainty sandwiches,
silver teapots and a trolley full of desserts.

In Britain in the 1840's, lunch was light and dinner
was not served until eight o'clock. Anna, the seventh
duchess of Bedford, decided to do something about
the weak, listless feeling she experienced every
afternoon. (Today we would call it low blood
sugar and eat a candy bar or a piece of fruit.)
Anna began having tea and cakes at five o'clock
and soon invited a few friends to join her.
Not a bad way to start such a wonderful tradition.

You will always stay young if you live honestly,
eat slowly, sleep sufficiently, work industriously,
worship faithfully – and lie about your age.
—Anonymous

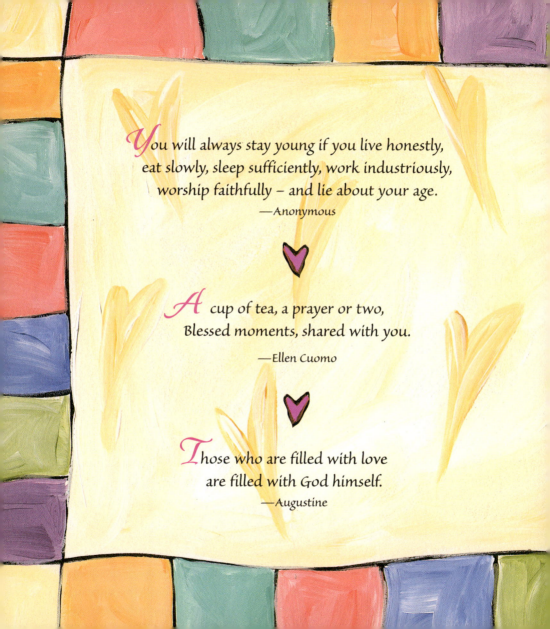

A cup of tea, a prayer or two,
Blessed moments, shared with you.

—Ellen Cuomo

*T*hose who are filled with love
are filled with God himself.
—Augustine

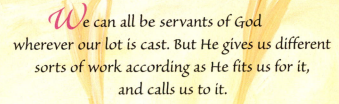

*W*e can all be servants of God
wherever our lot is cast. But He gives us different
sorts of work according as He fits us for it,
and calls us to it.

—George Eliot

*T*here can be no happiness equal to the joy of
finding a heart that understands.

—Victor Robinsall

A real friend is one who sticks by you, even
when you become successful.

—Anonymous

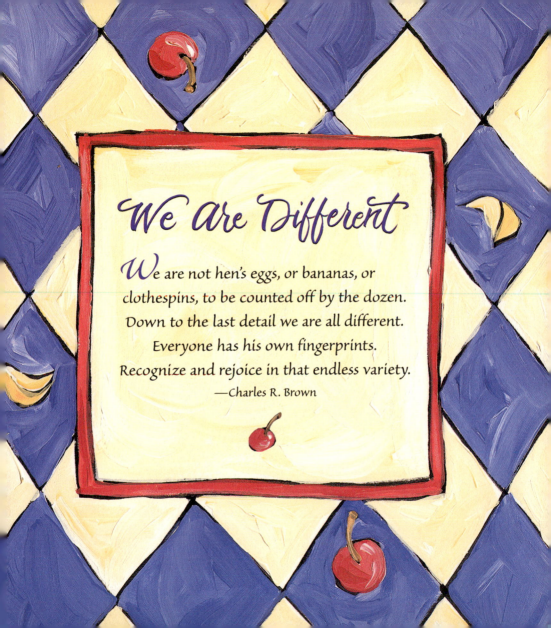

We Are Different

We are not hen's eggs, or bananas, or clothespins, to be counted off by the dozen. Down to the last detail we are all different. Everyone has his own fingerprints. Recognize and rejoice in that endless variety.

—Charles R. Brown

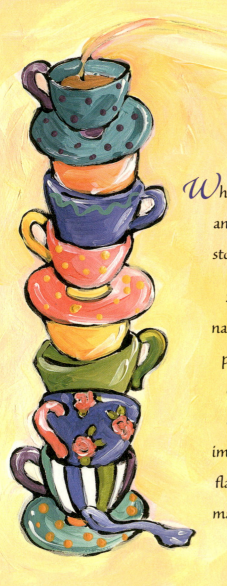

You Mean It's Also Healthy?

While most of us love tea for its pleasing flavor and calming effect, there is another side to the story. Tea is not only good, but is good for you!

Specifically: Tea contains phytochemicals – naturally occurring plant compounds that may play a positive role in helping the body fight certain cancers, maintaining healthy blood cholesterol levels and supporting a healthy immune system. Specific phytochemicals called flavonoids, found in both black and green tea, may have even stronger antioxidant properties than many fruits and vegetables...and antioxidants are believed to neutralize free radicals, which scientist believe may play a role in the development of chronic illnesses such as some types of cancer and heart disease.

Tea contains approximately the same amount of fluoride as fluoridated water. Drinking tea may help support healthy tooth enamel. Drinking tea plays a significant role in maintaining fluid balance, which is crucial for normal body function. Most adults need about two quarts of fluid daily, which should come from beverages and some fruits and vegetables. Therefore, go ahead. Have another cup or glass or bottle of tea. Here's to your health.

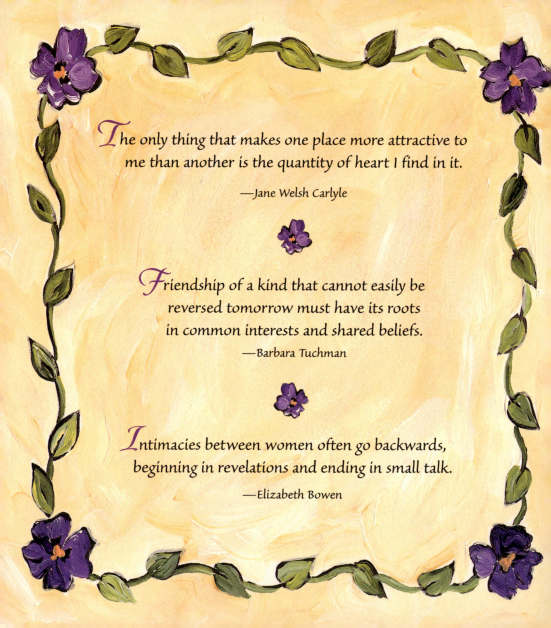

*T*he only thing that makes one place more attractive to
me than another is the quantity of heart I find in it.

—Jane Welsh Carlyle

*F*riendship of a kind that cannot easily be
reversed tomorrow must have its roots
in common interests and shared beliefs.

—Barbara Tuchman

*I*ntimacies between women often go backwards,
beginning in revelations and ending in small talk.

—Elizabeth Bowen

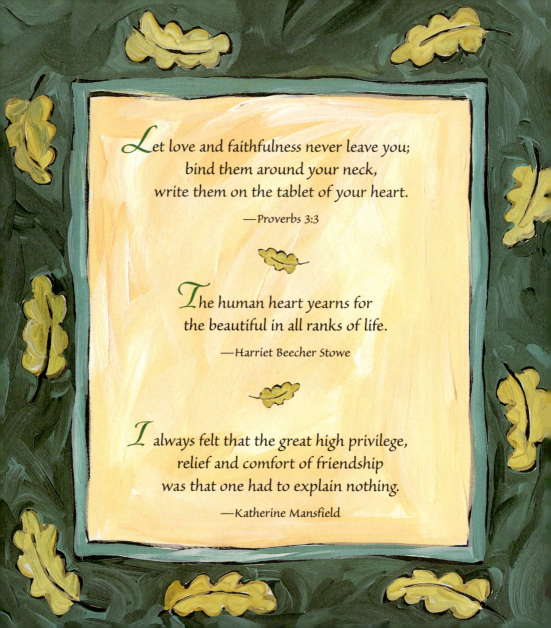

*L*et love and faithfulness never leave you;
bind them around your neck,
write them on the tablet of your heart.

—Proverbs 3:3

*T*he human heart yearns for
the beautiful in all ranks of life.

—Harriet Beecher Stowe

I always felt that the great high privilege,
relief and comfort of friendship
was that one had to explain nothing.

—Katherine Mansfield

Knowing You, Knowing Me

You understand what I have left unsaid.
You appreciate in me things I have long since
taken for granted. You suggest the improvements
I need to make for areas of my life I had written off
as hopeless. And you challenge me to use talents
I deny or help me see when I'm chasing pipe dreams.
You call me to higher aspirations that I can imagine
for myself and give me courage to try new things.
In knowing you, I no longer wonder who I really am
because, through you, I see my own dignity, honor
and worth. Through you I am able to overcome my
feelings of failure and weakness. In you I see
a clearer image of me. In knowing you, I know me.

—Mary Hollingsworth

*P*eople who have warm friends are healthier
and happier than those who have none.
A single real friend is a treasure worth
more than gold or precious stones.
Money can buy many things, good and evil.
All the wealth of the world could not buy you
a friend or pay you for the loss of one.

—G. D. Prentice

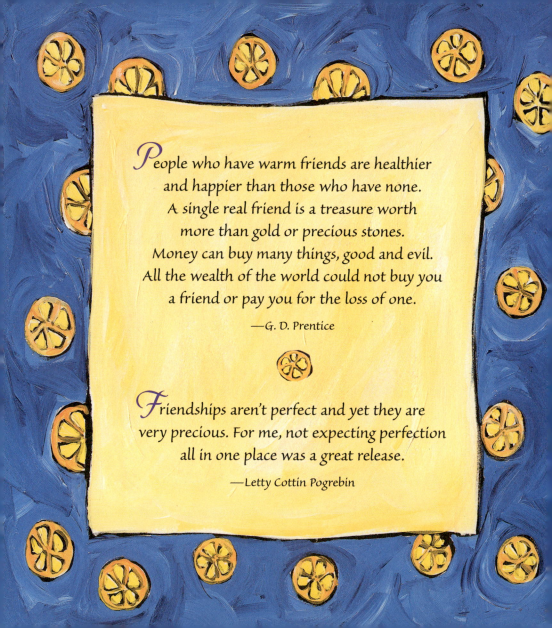

*F*riendships aren't perfect and yet they are
very precious. For me, not expecting perfection
all in one place was a great release.

—Letty Cottin Pogrebin

Tea or Ale?

*I*n the eighteenth century, tea became an institution, partly with a boost from Queen Anne, who reigned from 1702 to 1714. She started the custom of drinking tea instead of ale for breakfast. She is also credited with originating the use of a large silver teapot instead of the small Chinese ceramic ones.

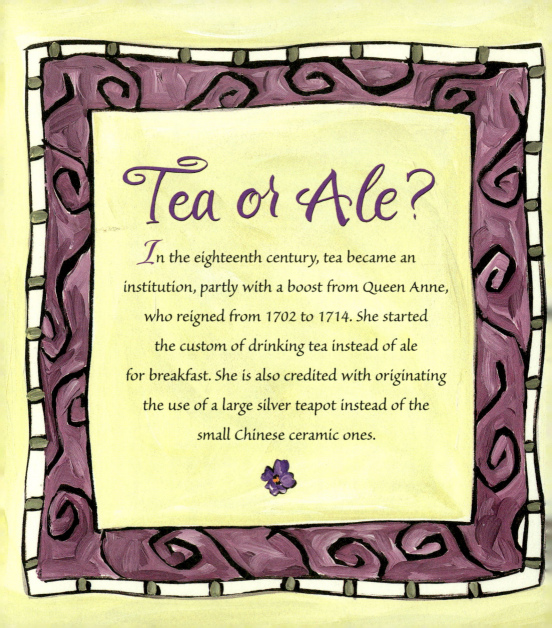

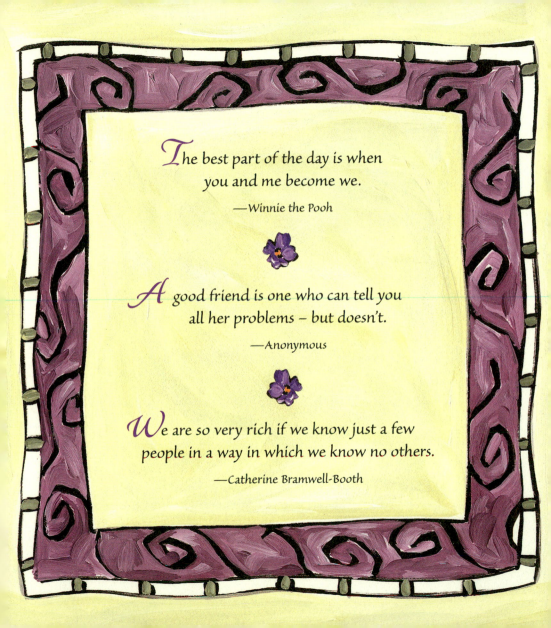

The best part of the day is when
you and me become we.

—Winnie the Pooh

A good friend is one who can tell you
all her problems – but doesn't.

—Anonymous

We are so very rich if we know just a few
people in a way in which we know no others.

—Catherine Bramwell-Booth

The greatest gift we can give one another is rapt attention to one another's existence.

—Sue Atchley Ebaugh

According to *Erh Ya*, an ancient Chinese dictionary dating back to 350 B.C., tea was cultivated commercially by the first century A.D. In the 1600s the Dutch opened tea plantations in Java and imported tea to Europe. Legend has it that the first tea to reach England arrived with a British admiral who had captured a Dutch ship and discovered the tea in its galley. Now tea is second only to water as the world's most popular drink, as well as the least expensive.

Be completely humble and gentle; be patient, bearing with one another in love.

—Ephesians 4:2

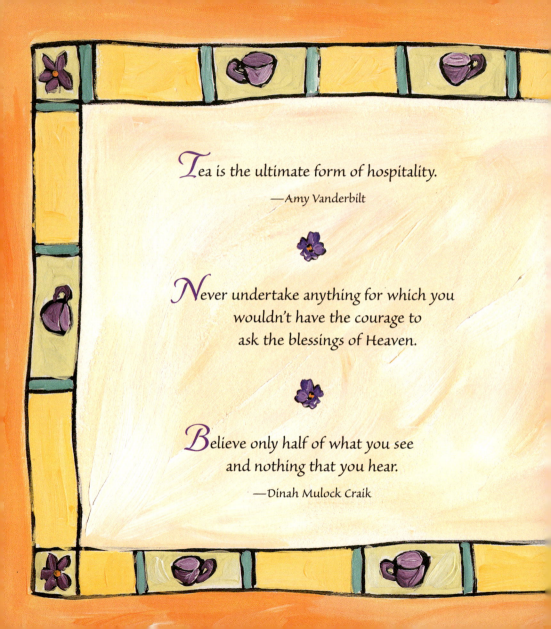

Tea is the ultimate form of hospitality.

—Amy Vanderbilt

*Never undertake anything for which you
wouldn't have the courage to
ask the blessings of Heaven.*

*Believe only half of what you see
and nothing that you hear.*

—Dinah Mulock Craik

Tea Conquers All

Did you know that the English were coffee drinkers when the East India Company began importing tea to England? Tea conquered the coffee habit in a few short years. But, dear as it became to the English, for the first hundred years tea was a novel treat only for the very rich. It wasn't until the close of the seventeenth century, when imports were up to 20,000 pounds a year, that enough tea was available for almost everyone to have a cup a day. When the English taste for tea outdid coffee and made a dent in the ale trade, Parliament levied tax on tea.

Despite the expense, tea was something the British could no longer live without.

The Cat Who Came to Tea

When the tea is brought at five o'clock,
And all the curtains are drawn with care,
The little black cat with bright green eyes
Is suddenly purring there.

—Harold Monro

Dreams come a size too big so
that we can grow into them.

—Josie Bissett

The Art of Tea

*W*here legend ends and fact begins is uncertain,
but it is generally accepted that the discovery of tea
occurred in ancient China. The Chinese say it was
their Emperor Shen-Nung in 2737 B.C. who first
tasted tea. The story goes that while he was boiling
his drinking water a few leaves from a wild tea bush
accidentally fell into the water. The Emperor liked
the delicate flavour they imparted to the water
and so the art of tea making was born.

The Story of Ceylon Tea